A Pocketful of Scars

Poems

by

Laird Lee Kirk

©2023
Lee Kirk
LJMcD Communications

ISBN: 9798370598074

Ipswich, Queensland, Australia

Contact LJMcD Communications:
lachlan.mcdougall@gmail.com

CONTENTS

Introduction

Laird Lee Kirk, as he likes to be known, is a Gregory Corso beat genius for the Scottish urban Twitter generation. His simple, forceful verse pushes into the abstract reaches of the everyday and brings out the sublime absurdity and the nascent hysteria that lingers there. Bubbling just under the surface of every poem is a quiet breakdown, a flood of humanity in the cold, detached voice of jaded youth.

This chapbook, these sixteen simple poems, speaks to a very real set of human experiences. Rooted firmly in the everyday, they pulse up in flowers at the most unexpected places. Perhaps Kirk has played the beats over in his own head as he was writing this, or perhaps he is naturally attuned to the sensitivities of an overabundance of life, but either way he has constructed a riveting suite of poems that deserve a thorough reading and a life of their own.

I hope you enjoy these poems as much as I have. I hope some of their convivial snark leaves a lasting impression and helps you to make sense of the lunacy of modern life. But most of all, I hope you read and enjoy as these poems are meant to be enjoyed. They are celebrations of humanity in all its flawed beauty and that is something worth enjoying.

Lachlan J McDougall

FIN

He was him dearly

Without sense

And is biblical dead.

EERIE ORANGES

Smooth and fine
tastes
like the best wrong

A caramac
melting on
chippy chips.

Eating
beef stew
with
marks and spencers
custard.

Makes
this aw richer
fulla
aw these
speckled lights
bringing
the
light bringer
who brought
backwards
into
forwards

into itself

at the same time
so dearly
loving

to aw

the contradictions
that makes
us loiter

like
pedestrian signals,

under
orange covers

waiting

for

the execution.

POEM CALLED BOO

Yesterday, I saw
the girl who
ghosted me

on Bumble
last week.

I nearly used
an ouija board
to find oot
why
those gorgeous
blue eyes

I said were
a million miles
decided on
naw.

None of my
business
anyway,

why you,
don't get
Captain
Beefheart.

She walked past
with the great
dane used
as the

profile pic.

Sniffing
at my feet

Kidding
On she
was, busy

with
her high-level
performance

looking
intently at
the pine trees
far away.

Here,
That means
I've been
ghosted
twice tae.

That felt
like
3, wee punches
to the stomach
Aw, at the same
time

but really
the more
it happens

the more
I get it

just sometimes
at that
peak.

Brings this
heat.
Changes
the mind.

And there's
no words

there is no
need to
say cheerio

But
it is,
cruel
as fuck,

even
if it's not
meant to be.

You're still
the arsehole.

Get this.

then I met someone
fae
OK CUPID.

An NHS nurse
who was six foot
4

and said she was
looking to
fuck
but not just a
one night
stand.

I ghosted
her
on the eve
of the meet.

And now.
I've turned
Casper:

The chickenshit ghost.

MAGNETIC SERVICE OF THE SEWN EMPRESS

Like
a late 1970s Disney illusion
with magick,
electricity
passing between
our lips
when kissing

on top of the lighthouse tower
looking over rooftops of the city centre,

I've swallowed
your mouth, enough
to hear
sweet thoughts.

but,
not all of them,
thank fuck.

When
I saw our reflection
on your bedroom mirror;
it was there.

A powerful/invisible
rhyme and rhythm.

What were the steps,
marching us through
all the seasons

past the
train wrecks,
car crashes of
of
other peoples lives

Something
bloomed from within
changing our feelings,
then it's
aw became a chore.

Even the
late nite phone calls,
255 bus journeys
that show up
in its own time

hangovers from
aw the
nasty arguments,
buttons
I never
knew I had
pressed too many times.

Pure ended,
up with
holes in my beard
and everything.

Fleetwood's song Everywhere,
played through
the speakers

shaped like refusing squirrels
at central station's pub,
looking out
the window past
her shoulder

aw the
passengers
on the platform

They looked like ice skaters
on the white-polished floor.

So picking up
a black bin bag
full of her
unironed clothes,
I arrived with

Noticed
on the picture,
to our left
as we were leaving

Three fat men lying
aw, drunk,
one is under a tap,
mouth wide open

drinking
aw the
alcohol pouring
from a wooden barrel.

Written above them
'Some dream, isn't it?'

It sure was, I said
to myself
walking her to the turnstile
of the underground station.

'I WANT HER TO LOVE YOU LIKE NOTHING'S EVER HAPPENED TO HER,'

It's

weird,

this

poem's

title

has

the feel

of

the tender

evening

hushed

anyway,

you get

to see

the ending.

He had been in

the room twice

already

but in

a previous manifestation:

destroyed

in an entire life

that was worshipped.

in public,

ceremony

robes

MORE PLEASE

More, please. A door chap is rare.

And it should not be, so is the nature reserve with all
the wildlife it houses halves the journey
to get the floor scraped I ordered online to collect at
store. Channel Tex recommended a
fine-looking one with fashioned steel the same colour
as Robocops head.

'Here. Have some meat?' said Maureen at the door
I decline as I let her walk past, pointing to Mum in
the kitchen.

'Ol Maureen with door chapping not heard since my
walkman chewed up Purple Rain tape
like crisps.

She handed me a packet of 1984. A wee flux
capacitor. Enchantment, fae under the sea.
That generation deserves its place, just a kind
reminder of decency, sophistication and no
such thing as class. They had class -
but there was no class, just equal. Nothing is ever
equal, but aye.

Whatever it was/is,

we need more of
please.

DOCTOR WHO STALKER

A big man
knitted
dr who scarfs

to
pass the
time

between
the twilight
calls

followed
me into
the toilet

when i
went
into aux 4

saying
hello again

as I
sat
in the
cubicle

escaping
the call
floor

when i
should
have
ignored

I shouted
'alright '
back

hearing
him
wash
his hands

had
a power
sleep
for
ten minutes

after i
flushed
the empty
bowl

opened
the door

the hand
dryer
switched
on

and

sure
enough

there
he was
standing

smiling
at
me

drying
his hands

the
same
smile

I saw
reflecting
in the
vending
machine

yesterday

getting
my bean
to cup
latte

men
are weird

when

they

are

horny

Masters of it.

LIVE FROM THE THETA STATE

A very sharp
corner,
there
was the dark

Stamped on it
the spirits
of expiry dates

clearly acting
aw wide
in world

of just light

being
undesirable
started
aw this caper.

"it's hard to take
away from people,
just a few things.
You get something
though'

said the

cloth people

in a dream

this morning,

just

think

tho

I've
seen that

you've no...

DEEP DIVER DIVING INSIDE YO'SELF

Alright,
I've kissed
men
on those
trigger lips

and the
women
I've hugged
unconditionally.

Advising,
their
antecedents
need fired.

Or it
will always
be there

aw that shite
passed down

It's
not yours.

Make,
your own Ire.

Made of
'Are we fuck
het for any

cunt

Glorious,
ferocious,

Of the rough,

nothing,
diamond-like
but

Tumbled stones,
used for walls

Keeping safe
against
that
shaky scaffolding

Of
that breed.
poised
status,

The salt
of the earth'ers,
saying

it's
getting evil early,

pray twice.

'MON THEN MOUNTAINS

Distant
mountains
on a
sinking island

looking at my
own back.

Back
from
what
was

and
what
is,

what
I did.

Anyway,

Nothing
but

a presence,

to an
angle
of 90 degrees,

black-figure

showing baby teeth,

the teeth
become
motorway

until a
Asda
truck ran
him
starboard,

He
was here.

There.

He became
everything
and older.

He is my hero
'cos everyone

was
his enemy.

I wish
I didn't care.

But now

my voice

is getting

bigger

Lay on

into

the rest

of my face

If you wish.

I could have
gotten used
to this

if it wasn't
for the
anger curling
the left
upper lip

feeling
like Elvis
foam,

just flat
infinite
glass
looking bone,

that when

destroyed
becomes
the blue ocean,

Waves
are the lips
of my silent
mouth,

invoking
the silence
where
we

aw
come from.

SHE'RA

Nothing
other,
than
this hold
on me

then,
the rose branches:

The rainfall
cleaning
my hair

Watching
them

holding hands
disappearing
into the fog.

walking down
to the
village bus stop

I saw
their faces
looking
into
my mind,

for they
have a long-lost voice

I felt when
I was a flower
in a lovely day
of past life.

of
concealed
danger

usually

caused
by the
exposure

of my body.

FROSTBITES

The cold air
had percolated
my thoughts

and it's not
small lamps
that lit the room

but the pale face
I feel looking
that I can't see

saying
there is

only
one
place

where you can
feel the blood
in your blood

and it's not
tonight.

and there's only
one place where

you can actually
see it.

but
more on
that later.

I have thoughts
to drink up.

I USED TO BE A MOUTH BREATHER

Since breathing
through my nose,
my face is
brighter

calmer

strong frown
had "gone

soft
evermore

I got into
my first morning
(actually about
1 hour and 15 minutes)

of the month
(with no rain)

with
stretching, press ups
to break the little
anxiety weight

from missing
my walk in the rain

watched a you tube
video how to
raindance

My eyes became blurry
from the raindrops
falling off the ceiling

to the skin of my neck.
i'm out of breath
from throwing
shapes

For this little cloud
that
thunderbolts me
something awful

Right in the adams
apple.

My hands seemed
to be spinning
involuntarily.

I could feel
my fingers

and toes

in the air

and
could hear my
earrings

scratching

and grinding
against the ground.

The world looked
better upside down.

THE MYTH OF WISDOM

I had to
take to it,

to find
the muscle

that
allows

it to work.

to put
everything

into new builds

with,
the same
cement isles

of a
thousand
revolutions
per cycle

all
the evolutions
per minute

everyone's
a different
tempo

individual
beats per minute

that's why
I don't
judge men/women

the world
don't move

to the beat
of one drum

what might
be right
for you
might not
be right
for some

what you
talking
about
Bruce Willis
is done?

He's
immortalised
in hard drives
from the VHS
days
of good
film covers

that
made me
feel safe

like
when in
haberdashery

hiding
fae it aw.

that

smoke

from
the

burnt
bridges

that held
me back
on saying

that
everything
will be
sentient
one day

and here
are the

days

even
windows
self-clean
after it rains.

this
awareness
that is
happening

decided to be
a part of
this poem,

after
being spliced
diced, cut up,
cut open
then pasted

into
online software
flushes
out

aw
different
stories,
of streets

emotional
geographies

that I wrote

tiny 'things
wee details
aw reversed

and now

it is looking
at you all

waiting
for your
eerie thumbs
to press
like.

cos it
can figure
oot an ending

to aw
this
Shite.

PEREO

Tastes buds scorched
from the butcher bought
Chinese pork

im eating
directly fae the
non-stick frying pan

in the darkness,
kitchen lights
oot.
looking from
my sister's window
toward the path that takes you
down to the underpass

watching for the
disembodied voices,
I heard shouting up when I...

anyway fuck plates

just eat from the spatula
go to the source it's remarkable

I know, I know
Billy Connoly had a bit about
the guy refusing to eat a fried egg
from a spatula

but, no
to brag

I've eaten
a full fry up
from the pan

bacon, and eggs
and two rostis which
look like crop circles

I picked directly
with my fingers,

dipped into the
salty yolk bursting
olive oil softly bubbled
softly bubbled

bubbly soft as
if like a sauce

I had a great time
with this
but after I realised

It's an omen for other types
of thing about
to happen.

It's not
bad or good,
like my horoscope
said, keep on your toes.

You have my thanks

and trust

that I do not leave
you in ignorance

Also, for the lack
of the
questioning the whole.

But aye, fuck plates.

NO NEED FOR ANYTHING FANCY

There are only two things
I want to happen.

Firstly
I used to go somewhere
on missions by myself.

Whenever I did go
it was in a
comfortable space.

All it looked like
was an
empty room

this wee place

but always
trees around

but you know
this
there's
always nature

in me words

but that's
just sometimes

That's where
I am now.

The only thing
I've
seen
strange

here

was
over there
before dawn.

I don't know
what it was
or is

it flashed
white
in the
corner
of my eye

as I
made
a circle
in a
circle
of trees

made
from the
broken
branches

like a tap

to the shoulder

showing
there is
so much
to earth

that
we
still don't
know

our parent(s)
were born
from liars

but that's
fine,

cos you
and I

are too

even, if
its no
meant

and further
I want to have an orgasm,

get the shower done in the morning

that the two i want.

well rested from
sweet sleep

dreaming
of
the mission

i did myself.

The only thing
seen is in this
vision

that strange thing

I've seen before

this time
I was
already

moving

faster

with both arms
in my hands.

but my teeth
were still
very clear.

Telling me

it

has

worked.

Laird Lee Kirk is a Laird of one square-foot centimetre grassland somewhere in Scotland.

He/him/who is a writer/poet/scribe creating portholes into ambient geographies of hazy broken human experiences sandwiched together like chalked black billboards.

Raw, honest, surreal and silly and most definitely hallucinatory form of fiction writing.

Other titles from LJMcD Communications:

- *The Audrey Adventures: A Collection of Erotic Stories* by J. Ollie Manoeuvre

- *The Further We Never Found* by Goran Tomic

- *Nagasaki Blues: A Hypernovel* by Lachlan J McDougall

All titles can be found on Amazon.com

COMMUNICATIONS

LACHLAN.MCDOUGALL@GMAIL.COM ···························· LINKTR.EE/LACHLAN_J_MCDOUGALL